...icultural mentor

...years.

...e this book a reality. Sue Gartley and Carol Stepanchuk
...leton for sharing Huichol stories and Carolyn Power for
...s for their support throughout the process. Also, thanks
...on Miller, Terry Bonnitt, Maria Medina, and St.
...ifornia. And to Nancy Ippolito, Pam Zumwalt, Bob
...and faith in this project.

...zanne Williams
...arfias Woo

..." Maiden," retold by Carolyn Power, San Francisco,

...LC 98-27409

...g Kong

...on Data

...lebrating Mexican festivals /
...llustrated by Yolanda Garfias Woo.

...d background, legends, recipes, crafts, and celebrations of

...iterature. 2. Mexico—Social life and customs—Juvenile
...ys—Mexico. 3. Mexico—Social life and customs.]
...olanda Garfias, ill. III.

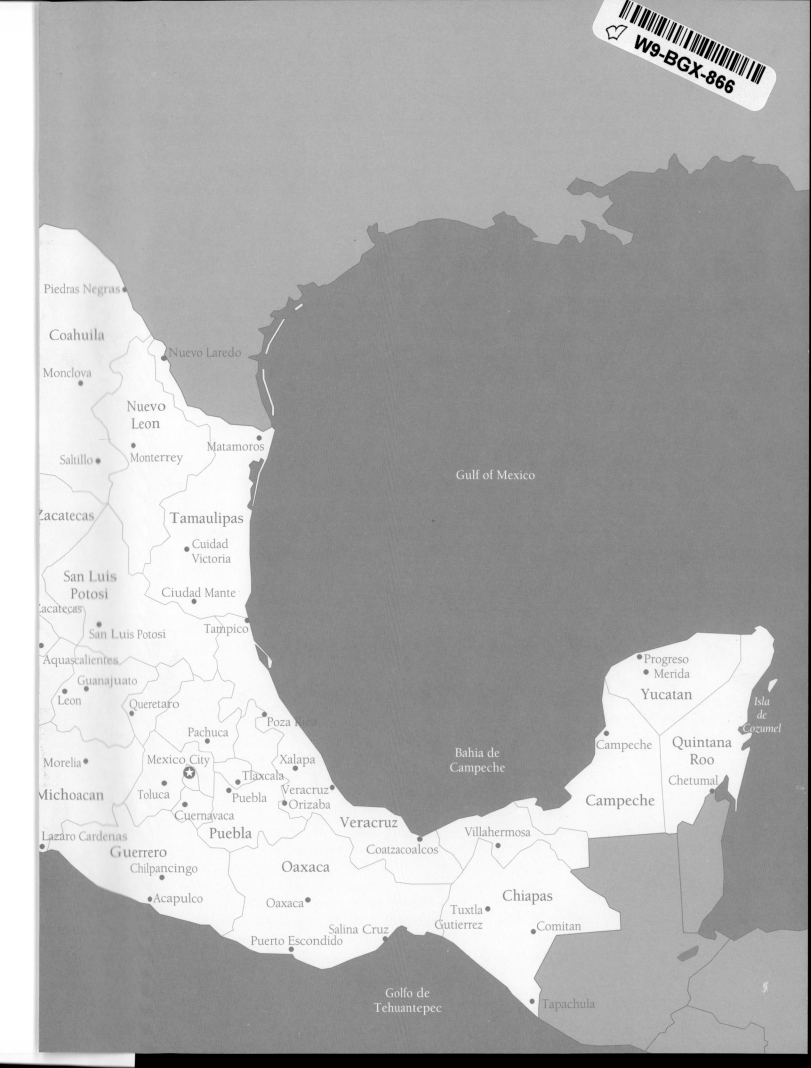

To Yolanda Garfias Woo, my mul[...]
and inspiration for the past thirty[...]
—Z.H.

To Graciela Tellez
—S.W.

For Gary and the artists of Mexi[...]
—Y.G.W.

Thank you to all the people who helped mak[...]
for their encouragement. Thanks to John Li[...]
retelling one, and to all our family and frien[...]
to Diane Romero de Ellis, Karl Danskin, Sha[...]
Michael's Catholic Church of Livermore, Ca[...]
Schildgen, and Mark Ong for their patience[...]

Text copyright © 1998 by Zoe Harris and Su[...]
Illustrations copyright © 1998 by Yolanda G[...]
Cover and text design by Mark Ong

Story on page 32, "Hungry Boy and the Cor[...]
California, storyteller (copyright © 1997).

Library of Congress Catalog Card Number:[...]
ISBN 1-881896-19-6

Printed in China by Twin Age Limited, Hor[...]

Library of Congress Cataloging-in-Publicat[...]
Harris, Zoe, 1941–
        Piñatas and smiling skeletons : c[...]
text by Zoe Harris and Suzanne Williams : [...]
                p.   cm.
        Summary: Examines the historic[...]
a year of special Mexican festivals.
        ISBN 1-881896-19-6
        1. Festivals—Mexico—Juvenile[...]
literature. [1. Festivals—Mexico. 2. Holid[...]
I. Williams, Suzanne, 1949–   . II. Woo, Y[...]
Title.
GT4814.A2H37   1998
394.26972—dc21
98-27409
CIP
AC

Contents

A Shower of Surprises

Thwack! Thunk! The **piñata** flies from side to side. "One more time!" children shout. The piñata is sure to break. What surprises are inside? A blindfolded boy swings his stick. Smack! The piñata splits and candy and toys shower down. Boys and girls dive and push, stuffing their pockets with treats.

Like a bright piñata, Mexico is full of surprises too. There are deserts in the north, volcanoes and broad valleys in the center, jungles in the south. In Mexico, you find parrots and whales, gila monsters and coyotes, coatis and monkeys. You can eat chicken in **mole** (a spicy chocolate sauce), fish **tacos**, hot chiles, or drink cool **agua de frutas** (a fruit drink).

Spanish is the main language but many Mexicans also speak languages of Mexico's original Indian people, the **indígenas**. Most Mexicans' ancestors include indígenas and Spanish colonists. Some people's ancestors came from other places, such as China, Germany, or Africa.

Some Mexicans live in villages, farming in traditional ways. Millions live in big, modern cities. Some Mexicans are rich. They may live in grand villas, drive fancy cars, and travel around the world. Some are middle class. They live comfortably. Many are poor. They may live without running water or electricity. Most, but not all, Mexicans are Catholics.

What do Mexicans have in common? Their land, their history, and their celebrations. Mexico has a lively mix of traditions from ancient indígena customs, and colonial Spaniards.

Every season has its own celebrations; each region its special traditions. Catholic holidays brought from Spain often include ancient ceremonies passed down from Aztec or Mayan cultures. Old Spanish customs have new additions. At Christmas, children hope for fashion dolls or Christmas trees as well as wooden toy **baleros** and piñatas. Even the Easter Bunny may appear in the plaza along with traditional dancers.

Mexicans say, "**somos muy festejeros**," (We like a good celebration). You can celebrate too. Fiestas are full of surprises. Like Mexico, or a piñata, they're overflowing with treats. **¡Qué vivan las fiestas!** Long live fiestas!

Old Gods and New Visions

Middle Americans shared common ideas. Most Middle Americans used the complex Mayan calendar. It had two sets of dates, one for ordinary days and one for sacred days. They wrote books, called **codices**, with pictographs (picture writing). New gods joined older ones as time passed. Some groups thought certain gods were more important than others. Gods were connected to certain places—mountains, valleys, or towns. People in those places claimed the gods as their special protectors and the land itself became sacred.

If you visit Mexico, you may see giant stone heads along the east coast, ancient cities in jungles and mountains, and sculptures of strange and beautiful gods worshipped long ago. The cities have broad streets, plazas, ball courts, and pyramids to honor gods. There are market places, temples, and palaces. Carvings of Quetzalcóatl, Tláloc, and Huitzilopochtli, gods of Aztecs and other ancient Middle Americans, peer out from temple walls. Who built these great cities? Where did they come from? Where did they go?

People have lived in Mexico for at least 10,000 years. Over the centuries many groups controlled different parts of the land. The ancient cities you can visit today were built at different times by different people . . . Mayans, Zapotecs, Tarascans, Toltecs, and Aztecs.

The giant heads of the east coast were carved around 3,000 years ago by people called Olmecs. They worshipped a jaguar god, Tláloc, and believed in human sacrifice. Their religious ideas spread throughout Middle America, changing the way many other groups thought.

Between A.D. 1 and 1000, Middle American cities such as the Mayans' Palenque and the Zapotecs' Monte Albán were centers of culture and power. Teotihuacán was the heart of the Mexican Valley between A.D. 300 and 750. How this grand city was destroyed and why its people disappeared is still a mystery.

Between A.D. 800 and 900 there was a terrible drought. People from the north poured into fertile Central Mexico looking for food. The immigrants spoke several forms of the Náhuatl language. Like the Olmec, Mayan, and other Mexican people, they believed gods demanded their most precious gift, human blood, to keep the world running smoothly. They often captured victims for sacrifice in war. A Náhuatl tribe, the Toltecs, controlled the Central Mexican Valley between A.D. 1000 and 1150. One of the last Náhuatl groups to arrive, the Mexicas (known today as Aztecs), settled in the marshes around Lake Texcoco about A.D. 1325. They lacked farm land so they built floating fields, **chinampas**, from mud and reeds. They built causeways and canals, and filled marshes. Their capital, Tenochtitlán, grew to a magnificent city of plazas, bridges, and canals. Aztecs were fierce fighters. They won land, sacrificial victims, and trading partners throughout the Valley. By 1519, Aztecs controlled most of central Mexico, almost 15 million people and 500 cities.

1519, named *One Reed* in the Middle American calendar, was the end of their 52-year calendar cycle. It was a dangerous year. Aztecs believed the sun had to be restarted on its journey after each cycle. Their priests predicted that Quetzalcóatl, the white plumed-serpent god, would return in 1519 to destroy the world they knew. It was the year Hernán Cortés landed in Mexico.

The white strangers arrived in huge boats, riding terrifying four-legged creatures (horses). Many indígenas were afraid. Armed with the legend, cannons, and thousands of local people eager to overthrow their old enemy, Cortés conquered the Aztec Empire after a tough, bloody war.

The Spanish destroyed Aztec government, killed their leaders, and toppled their gods. The invaders leveled their cities and divided their land among Spanish overseers. The Mexican people paid tribute (taxes) to the new conquerors in the same way they did the old ones. But their way of life, based on reverence to their gods and obedience to their priest-leaders, was shattered. Everything they believed in was gone.

The new Spanish colonists built European-style palaces, churches, and plazas where the great boulevards and temples of Tenochtitlán had stood. They burned indígena books and documents and used the stones of Aztec temples and palaces to build "New Spain." Noblemen and adventurers arrived to rule the land, make money for themselves, and send silver and gold to the king of Spain. Priests came to instruct the Mexican people in Spanish language, ways, and religion. Spain ruled Mexico for 300 years.

But instead of creating another Spain, the indígena culture and the Spanish culture blended. Old gods of villages were turned into Spanish saints. Dances and celebrations got new names. Spanish religion, clothing, and fiestas substituted for ancient ones. Today, Mexican celebrations are a glorious mix of the old and the new, the indígena and the Spanish.

Alligator — Cipactli

Wind — Ehecatl

House — Calli

Lizard — Cuetzpallin

Serpent — Coatl

Death — Miquiztli

Deer — Mazatl

Rabbit — Tochtli

Water — Atl

Dog — Itzcuintli

Monkey — Ozomatli

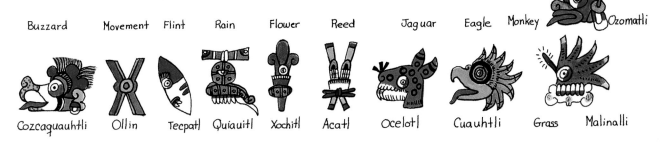

Buzzard — Cozcaquauhtli

Movement — Ollin

Flint — Tecpatl

Rain — Quiauitl

Flower — Xochitl

Reed — Acatl

Jaguar — Ocelotl

Eagle — Cuauhtli

Grass — Malinalli

Creation

There is no one story of creation from Mexico. When the Spanish burned indígena codices they destroyed the records of indígena religion. Still, we know Middle Americans were religious people who, through thousands of years and different empires, kept old gods and beliefs while adding new ones. Most Middle Americans believed the universe began with one god. The god had two sides—male and female, earth and water, dark and light. Its Náhuatl name was Ometeotl. Ometeotl had four sons: Tlatlauhqui Tezcatlipoca (Red Smoking Mirror), Yayauhqui Tezcatlipoca (Black Smoking Mirror), Quetzalcóatl (Feathered Serpent), and Huitzilopochtli (Blue Hummingbird). Quetzalcóatl and Huitzilopochtli created fire, a weak sun, and the first man and woman. They divided time into days and created the Place of the Dead.

Some legends say the earth was made like this: together, all four brothers made Tláloc, the god of water, and his wife. From the new water, the earth goddess, Tlalteotl, appeared. When Quetzalcóatl and Tezcatlipoca saw her, they turned themselves into serpents and dove into the water. They tore the earth goddess to pieces. Half of her became the earth, the other half the sky.

But the other gods were angry. To make up for hurting Tlalteotl, Quetzalcóatl and Tezcatlipoca made trees and flowers from her hair, grass from her skin, wells and rivers from her many eyes. Her head became the moon and her shoulders the mountains.

Middle Americans believed the gods created and destroyed the sun and earth four or five times. Each sun the gods made was different. One was a weak Water Sun. At the end of that age, the gods leveled the earth with a huge flood and turned the people into fish. The next suns were suns of Air, Fire, and Earth. Gods destroyed these suns too and ruined the earth with wind or fire. They changed people into birds and monkeys. Sometimes a couple escaped and became the parents of the next age of people. Aztecs believed they lived under the Fifth Sun. They predicted the time of the Fifth Sun would end with hunger and earthquakes. Quetzalcóatl would return to Tenochtítlan from the east. Then their world would end in ruin.

Middle Americans believed time repeated itself each time the sun was reborn. To them, time didn't march forward. Time moved in a circle. The centuries formed a long cycle of predictable events, then started over again.

Tlatlauhqui Tezcatlipoca

Ometeotl

Yayauhqui Tezcatlipoca

Quetzalcóatl

Huitzilopochtli

Tláloc

Tlatleotl

La Virgen de Guadalupe

The Virgin of Guadalupe

In December 1531, 12 years after Spanish soldiers conquered the land, something happened that helped Spanish priests win the Mexican people's hearts.

The story goes like this: Juan Diego, a young indígena went walking on the Hill of Tepeyac. It was a sacred place for Aztecs. They traveled to Tepeyac to worship Tonantzin, the mountain-mother, water-mother, the Mother of All Gods. Tepeyac was her special place.

Juan Diego heard sweet music and saw a young woman, dark-skinned and black-haired like indígena people. Was she Tonantzin? No, she was the Virgin Mary, Mother of Jesus, from the Spanish faith. A miracle! The Virgin told him to tell the Catholic bishop to build a church at the place she appeared. Juan Diego ran to the Bishop with her message, but the Bishop didn't believe him.

Juan Diego saw the Virgin Mary again. She told him to climb Tepeyac hill and gather a bouquet of flowers. Juan Diego didn't argue although he knew, in December, no flowers could grow on the cold, rocky hill. But when he reached the top, it was filled with flowers! Juan Diego wrapped a bunch in his **tilma** (cloak) and carried them to the Bishop. When the Bishop unwrapped the flowers, a picture of the Virgin appeared on Juan Diego's tilma. Another miracle! The Bishop was convinced Juan Diego had seen the Virgin.

Today you can see Juan Diego's tilma at the Basilica of the Virgin of Guadalupe, on the hill of Tepeyac, in Mexico City. The colors of her image have not faded with time. The 46 stars in the picture are in the exact positions of the constellations during the winter solstice (December 21) in 1531. All Mexicans know about La Virgen de Guadalupe. She has become their symbol of peace, justice, and national pride.

People have argued for 400 years about the truth of the story of La Virgen de Guadalupe. But still there is no doubt millions of Mexicans love her and believe in her. December 12, El Día de la Virgen de Guadalupe, has been a national holiday in Mexico since 1859.

El Día de la Virgen de Guadalupe

Mariachis play traditional Mexican music. The musicians play guitars, *guitarrones* (big bass guitars), violins, and sometimes trumpets. They are usually men. Mariachis wear sombreros, and suits decorated with silver buttons. Most Mexican cities have a place, a park or hall, where mariachi bands meet and play, waiting to be hired to work at a fiesta or wedding.

The morning is cool. The sun is just rising. Thousands of people from all over Mexico crowd toward the Basilica of the Virgin of Guadalupe outside Mexico City. The **peregrinos** (pilgrims), come with families, friends, or soccer teams. Groups of merchants, carpenters, or teachers travel together. Everyone carries flowers . . . from small bouquets to 40-foot-high arrangements. Vendors sell all kinds of food and clothes. Some groups return year after year, as their parents and grandparents did, to play music and dance for the Virgin. As they approach the church, some pilgrims kneel and walk the last hundred yards across the stone square on their knees.

Every year over 12 million people visit the Basilica at the place where La Virgen appeared. The biggest crowds fill the plaza on December 12, the Feast of La Virgen de Guadalupe. This is a day for celebrating throughout Mexico. Churches dedicated to La Virgen de Guadalupe have special festivities. Neighbors get together to build altars of flowers for her. They go to mass, then dance and celebrate to mariachi music. Families may have a special dinner. In Guadalajara, vendors line the square outside the church selling **buñuelos** (sweet sticky bread), **raspados** (fruit ices), and **tortas** (cakes). There are bullfights, rodeos, and parades. El Día de la Virgen de Guadalupe is a truly Mexican celebration.

Buñuelos
Sweet Fried Bread

Buñuelos are a traditional holiday treat. Ask an adult to help you make some.

> 2 cups flour
> 1 tablespoon sugar
> ½ teaspoon baking powder
> 1 teaspoon salt
> 1 egg
> ⅜ cup milk
> ⅛ cup (¼ stick) butter, melted
> ¼ cup sugar, mixed with 2 teaspoons
>   cinnamon for sprinkling
> cooking oil for frying—enough for about
>   one inch in a heavy frying pan

Sift together the flour, sugar, baking powder, and salt. In another bowl, beat the eggs. Add the milk and butter, then the flour, beating after each addition. The dough should be soft so that it can be kneaded. Turn it onto a floured board and knead the dough until smooth (add a little flour if it is too sticky). Divide it into 24 pieces. Shape them into balls and let stand for 20 minutes.

Then, using a floured rolling pin, flatten each ball into a circle about 6 inches across. Heat the oil to about 350°. Fry, one or two at a time, turning once, until light brown. Drain on paper towels. Sprinkle with sugar-cinnamon mix.

Paper Flowers

Mexicans decorate with bunches of fresh or paper flowers throughout the year.

You will need tissue paper, pipe cleaners, floral or masking tape, scissors, and a hole punch.

Cut two 3-inch × 24-inch strips of tissue paper. Put 2 strips together and fold in half lengthwise and in half again. Now you will have a 3 × 6-inch rectangle (8 layers thick).

Without unfolding the paper, cut a pattern for flower petals as shown (1) (or make up your own pattern). Unfold the last fold so you have 4 layers of tissue. Slide the middle two layers of tissue so the petals are not directly behind each other. Punch holes about every 2 inches through all layers (2). Then thread a pipe cleaner through the holes as though you are sewing.

Push the petals together toward the center of the pipe cleaner. Fold the pipe cleaner in half and twist tightly at the bottom of the petals. Hold the pipe cleaner together at the base of the petals. Cut about 8 inches of tape (masking or florist tape works best) and wind it tightly around the bottom of the flower and then around both pipe cleaners to make the stem (3). Trim.

Gently separate tissue layers and fluff petals to finish your flower.

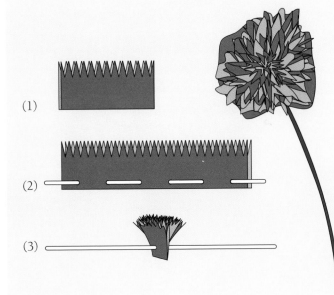

La Navidad

Christmas

It is the Christmas season. Mexican children have so much to look forward to . . . **Niño Jesús** (Baby Jesus) and piñatas, candlelight processions and holiday markets, gifts from the three kings and 12 special grapes. Winter holidays start with El Día de La Virgen de Guadalupe, December 12, and continue through Christmas, New Year's, **El Día de los Tres Reyes** (Three Kings' Day), January 6, and **Candelaria**, February 2. Each week brings new excitement. December 16–24 are the nights of the **posada**.

Children dress as **María, José**, and los peregrinos. Families and townspeople meet each night to act out Mary and Joseph's trip to Bethlehem. They light candles and walk from house to house. At each stop, they ask if there is room for them at the inn (posada). The answer is always *no*. Until, every night, the owner of the last house invites them in. They arrange their candles and lanterns around a nativity scene, then eat and celebrate together. The last house on Christmas Eve is the best . . . then children finish the posada by breaking a piñata decorated like the Star of Bethlehem.

Mexican American communities throughout the United States celebrate posadas too. Everyone is welcome to join the large processions sponsored by community groups in Chicago, San Antonio, Los Angeles, and other cities.

In Vera Cruz on Christmas Eve, people celebrate **La Rama.** They tie little clay statues of donkeys, shepherds, and angels on a tree branch. They decorate it with paper chains, ribbons, and Japanese lanterns. When La Rama, the branch, is ready, they go from house to house singing. "Give me my gift if you are going to. The night is long and we have far to go." People give the singers **aguinaldos,** small gifts of candy or fruit, and are thanked with another verse of the song.

In Oaxaca, sometimes there are three piñatas at the end of posada. One is filled with fruit and candy, one with flour, and one with water. No one knows which one is which!

La Noche Buena

Christmas Eve

Flor de la Noche Buena (Flower of the Blessed Night), the poinsettia, grows naturally in Mexico. Aztecs believed it stood for purity. After the Spanish conquest, a new legend appeared about a poor girl who needed a gift for Niño Jesús. Her gift, a plain bush, was miraculously transformed into the bright red Flor de la Noche Buena. The Mexican flower was carried to the Philippines by traders traveling between the two Spanish colonies. A similar legend is told there.

Pine needles are sprinkled on the floor. Every footstep crushes them, releasing their clean perfume. The house smells sweet like fruit. There is fruit for the piñatas and fruit for the punch. And, of course, there is candy. Christmas is coming. On the days before **La Noche Buena** (Christmas Eve) and **La Navidad** (Christmas), Mexicans are busy. They mix filling for tamales, fry buñuelos, stuff piñatas, and decorate churches and squares. Children try on their costumes for Las Posadas and set up **nacimientos** (nativity scenes) in their homes. People build nativity scenes in **zócalos** (town squares) and churches. Special markets sell all kinds of nacimientos. Most nacimientos stay up from December 16 through January 6 (Three Kings' Day).

People in Oaxaca make nacimientos from radishes! These scenes last only one day, December 23, **La Noche de los Rábanos** (Night of the Radishes). People carve intricate sculptures of shepherds, angels, plants, and animals. Of course, nacimientos include the Holy Family—Jesús, María, and José. Artists carefully display their radish creations in the zócalo. On La Noche de los Rábanos, there are fireworks, music, and prizes for the best carving. Everyone eats buñuelos, then smashes his or her plate on the ground for good luck.

On December 24, La Noche Buena, people gather in front of the church. Figures of María and José wait at the manger. The people line up behind a figure of Niño Jesús, singing and bringing gifts for him. Children wait eagerly to join the candlelight procession into the church. Then they stay for midnight mass.

Christmas is a quiet day. Children traditionally receive gifts on January 6, Three Kings' Day. Customs change, and now Mexican children may get gifts on Christmas Day. Either way, La Navidad is a day for church and family.

Año Nuevo, El Día de los Tres Reyes, y Candelaria

New Year's, Three Kings' Day, and Candelmas

December 31 is **El Día de Gracias,** or Thanksgiving. People go to church to give thanks for their blessings. City families celebrate New Year's Eve with a special dinner. Dessert is **canastillas con las doce uvas,** baskets of 12 grapes. At midnight, they play a game. Each person eats one grape at each of the 12 strokes of the clock. If you eat all twelve grapes before the clock stops ringing, you'll have good luck. If you are single, you will be married in the coming year! **¡Próspero Año! ¡Feliz Año Nuevo!** Happy New Year!

After New Year's comes another holiday children love. They fill their shoes with hay and line them neatly on the doorstep. The hay is for the camels. Whose camels? The Three Kings'! Children in Mexico write letters to the Kings asking for gifts, then put the letters and the shoes out on January 5 for the Kings. The Kings "arrive" on the sixth, El Día de los Tres Reyes. The kings fill shoes with candy and leave gifts for children.

On El Día de los Tres Reyes, there may be another party with a piñata, or a parade led by boys on horseback dressed as the Kings. There is sure to be hot chocolate and sticky **rosca de reyes,** sweet bread filled with candied fruits and nuts. Some lucky person finds a tiny doll (Niño Jesús) baked inside the bread. The person who finds the doll gives a party on Candelaria, February 2.

Candelaria is the last celebration of La Navidad. It may be celebrated with more parades, rodeos, or special dances. People light a **castillo** (castle) frame covered with firecrackers. They launch **cohetes** (firework rockets). Late in the day, a girl chosen as **comadre** (godmother) ceremoniously takes Niño Jesús from the manger and dresses him in new clothes. The figure is blessed, and the nacimiento put away, ending the long, joyous season.

The calendar used throughout ancient Middle America had eighteen 20-day months . . . 360 days. It ended with five unlucky left-over days. A second, "sacred" calendar lasted 260 days. Every 52 years (bundle of years) both calendars started together. This was a time of change and danger. Mayans also used a "long" calendar which may have been 9 million years long!

Luminarias

When you approach the New Mexican village, Velarde, on Christmas Eve, turn out your headlights. The highway into town is lined with hundreds of glowing **luminarias** . . . candles protected by paper bags. With the Rio Grande on one side and steep mountains on the other, the road to Velarde is **encantado** (enchanted) tonight.

Luminarias, or **farolitos**, represent campfires the shepherds lit as they traveled to find Niño Jesús. Mexicans, who had settled along the Rio Grande, honored this tradition.

Now at Christmas time, New Mexican houses, businesses, streets, and plazas glitter with luminarias. Luminarias line quiet streets in Phoenix, Santa Fe, or Los Angeles. You can even buy luminaria bags decorated with stars or Christmas trees.

¡Feliz Navidad!

Posada Song

This is a song Mexican Children sing during Posada:

En el nombre del cielo os pido posada, pues no puede andar mi esposa amada.	In the name of heaven we beg you let us stay, my dear wife cannot walk any farther today.
Aquí no es mesón, *sigan adelante,* *yo no puedo abrir* *no sea algun tunante.*	*This is not a hotel,* *keep moving on, I say,* *you might be a thief,* *you must go away.*
Mi esposa es María, la Reina del Cielo y Madre va a ser del Divino Verbo.	My wife is María, Queen of Heaven and Earth, she'll soon be the mother of God's most Divine Word.
Entren santos peregrinos, *reciben este rincón* *aunque es pobre la morada* *es grande mi corazón.*	*Come in holy pilgrims* *rest in our small space,* *the house may be poor* *but kind hearts fill this place.*
Humildes peregrinos, Jesús, María, y José, mi alma doy con ellos, mi corazón también.	To the three humble pilgrims, Jesús, María, y José, I give to them my soul and my heart on this day.

Biscochitos
Anise Seed Christmas Cookies From New Mexico

3 cups flour
1½ teaspoons baking powder
½ teaspoon salt
1 cup shortening (or ½ cup butter, ½ cup shortening)
½ cup sugar
1 egg
1 teaspoon anise seeds
3 tablespoons water
¼ cup sugar mixed with 2 teaspoons cinnamon for sprinkling

Preheat oven to 350 degrees. Sift flour, baking powder, and salt together. In another bowl, cream sugar and shortening. Add the egg and anise seeds to the sugar mixture and and beat again. Add about half the flour mixture to the egg-sugar mixture, and beat in. Add the rest of the flour. Mix again, while adding enough of the water to hold the dough together. You may not need all the water. Chill the dough in the refrigerator for about an hour.

Roll the dough out on a floured board or between two pieces of waxed paper to about a quarter inch thick. Cut it into fancy shapes. Place cookies onto a lightly greased baking sheet. Sprinkle with the sugar-cinnamon mix. Bake for 10–12 minutes, until light brown. Cool on rack.

Aguinaldos
Special Christmas Gifts

Mexican children might get **aguinaldos** on Christmas day, New Year's Eve, or in their shoes on Three Kings' Day.

To make aguinaldos you need toilet-tissue or paper-towel rolls, tissue or crepe paper, ribbon or yarn, and fillings (coins, candies, small fruits or toys).

First, tuck the fillings inside the tube. Then, wrap the rolls in bright paper. Tie the ends with ribbon or yarn. Decorate the outside of the aguinaldo with paper cut-outs, or glitter.

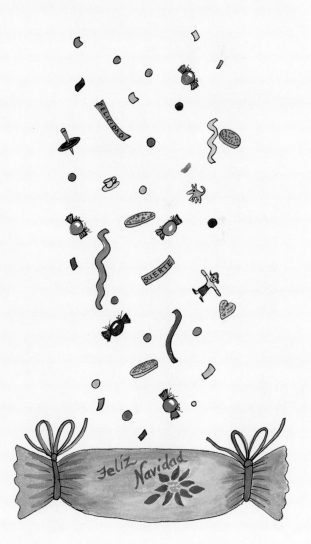

Carnaval

The masks are ready. The glass eyes are polished and the pink, Spanish-looking cheeks painted. A child runs his fingers over the bright yellow face of a jaguar. The wooden mask feels smooth and cold. He strokes the ridges above the eyes, the line of the nose. The mask seems alive. He watches the mask maker finish his work. The boy learns. One day, maybe he will carve powerful masks. He knows that regular people change when they wear these masks. Behind the wild faces, friends and relatives turn into eagles, serpents, or saints. The masks are magical.

The boy walks with his family to the square. Now the dancers and the townspeople take over. Today things will be backwards. In his village in the state of Hidalgo, old people dress as young ones, young as old, men dress up as women. The dance begins. "Watch closely," his mother says. He does. When he's older, he'll dance too.

In another town, in the state of Tlaxcala, **charros** (cowboy dancers) entertain the crowd. Meanwhile, dancers called **paragüeros**, or umbrella salesmen, prepare to dance with open umbrellas because they get so little rain. These umbrellas wouldn't keep them dry anyway. The paragüeros' umbrellas are made from giant feathers! In village after village, dancers perform. In the city of Mérida, Yucatán, children, families, school and community groups make costumes and march in a parade. The ceremonies are different, but the celebration is the same. It is Carnaval in Mexico.

Carnaval is celebrated in the days before Lent (the 40 days before Easter). In the Catholic religion, Lent is a time to think seriously about your life. People often give up favorite foods or hobbies. There are plays about the last days of Jesus' life and his crucifixion. Lent is a serious season.

No wonder people around the world have huge parties before it starts. European Catholics brought Carnaval to Mexico and indígenas added their traditions to the Carnaval parties. Masks and fireworks, dancing and bullfighting, praying and playing make Carnaval a special Mexican way to welcome spring.

The last week in Lent is **Semana Santa**, Holy Week. Mexicans, like Catholics around the world, have religious ceremonies throughout the week, ending with Easter Sunday. On Saturday before Easter, some communities burn Judas figures. People hang huge paper or straw figures of Judas, the disciple who betrayed Jesus, from trees or lamp posts. The figure is covered with candies, coins, and firecrackers. Children gather. They light the figure and treats rain down as Judas burns, twists, and explodes. Nowadays, people often break a Judas-shaped piñata instead. It's safer!

During Carnaval, dancers in Chiapas dress in monkey-fur hats, European-style coats, and special sandals that look like ones in ancient Mayan carvings. Called **Maash**, these Monkey Men lead the villagers in music, dancing, and finally a parade that ends at the church. There, they thank the Mayan sun god, Totik.

Tláloc, the Rain God

Tláloc, the Jaguar-toothed rain god, is one of the oldest gods of Middle America. He was first worshipped in Mexico by the Olmecs. Most later Middle American groups honored Tláloc too. The rain dances in Tlaxcala began in Aztec times when people spent the first 20 days of their year honoring rain and water gods such as Tláloc. Now the dances are part of Carnaval.

Corn Legends

Corn has always fed Mexicans. Ancient people planted corn and prayed to the rain gods to water it. The Mayans believed they were created from corn. The gods tried to make people three times. The first time they made them from mud. But the people were brittle and couldn't speak. The second try they made people from wood. These people had no blood and no feelings, so the gods destroyed them. The third time they shaped the people from corn flour mixed with the blood of the gods. These people were strong and had feelings. They became Mayans, children of corn.

Mexicans always worried it might not rain. Drought ruined crops and forced whole groups of people to move or die. One legend blames the ruin of Toltec civilization in A.D. 1150 on a ball game. The last lord of the Toltecs, Huemac, played a sacred ball game with Tláloc, the rain god. Huemac won and Tláloc offered him corn as a prize. But Huemac didn't want simple corn. He demanded jade and valuable feathers instead. Tláloc gave him the riches, but he warned, "Corn is easier to eat than cold stone!" Soon, there was a terrible drought. Huemac's people starved. The treasure was useless when there was no corn.

Battle of the Cascarones

Mexican children play Battle of the **Cascarones** (egg shells) during Carnaval. They form two lines. At a signal, they walk past each other, trying to break eggs on each other's heads. They end up covered with confetti, not raw eggs! That's because they use special cascarones. You can make them too:

Lightly tap a small hole in each end of a raw egg's shell and blow out the contents into a bowl. Rinse the empty eggshell and let it dry. Fill the eggshell with confetti. You may have to make one hole bigger. (Make confetti by cutting tiny pieces of colored paper).

Glue a piece of paper across each hole to seal it. Decorate the eggs with paint, markers, or colored tissue paper.

Now arm yourself with cascarones, line up, and let the battle begin!

Cascarones are used in the United States too. Since the 1500s, La Danza de las Cascarones has been held each spring in Santa Fe, New Mexico. Men buy beautiful cascarones and then invite women to dance by cracking the eggs over their heads. The one with the most confetti in her hair is the most popular!

Making Masks

Mexicans make masks of the jaguar, eagle, coyote, or other special animals. There are masks of gods such as Quetzalcóatl or Tláloc. There are masks for saints and Spanish soldiers. Masks may help tell a story or teach a lesson. Each region of Mexico has its own style of masks. Artists throughout Mexico put a lot of thought and creativity into making fabulous masks.

Make your own mask. Make it wild, scary, or fun. Mask makers take time to think about the animal or person the mask will represent before they begin. This is an important part of designing the mask. If you are making a jaguar mask, close your eyes and think like a jaguar. Feel like a jaguar. Imagine what he sees from his eyes. What does his face look like? What color is he? Is he strong or gentle? Now begin your mask. Use a paper plate, paper bag, cardboard, or papier mâché base. Decorate it with paint, feathers, sequins, glitter, pipe cleaners, ribbon, or yarn. Try using raffia or paper flowers. Make a box to save beads, papers, scraps of ribbons and yarn for your masks. Imagine, create, have fun!

Celebrating Beginnings

The family is the center of Mexican life. Grandparents, parents, uncles and aunts and children may live together in different parts of a large house or group of houses. Even if they don't live together, they celebrate together. Children are taught to honor their parents and grandparents. Parents may decide what children will study or if they will work. Children often work side by side with older relatives to learn the family trade or craft. Children must take their parents' wishes seriously. Parents work hard to love and provide for their families. Children take care of aging grandparents.

Everyone loves birthdays. Children in Mexico may have a birthday party, but they are just as likely to celebrate their Saint's Day. This is the day the Catholic Church honors the saint whose name they have. A boy named José celebrates the Day of St. Joseph (March 19). Isabela celebrates on St. Elizabeth's Day (July 8). The same goes for María (Mary), Pedro (Peter), Jorge (George), or Luisa (Louise). On Saint's Days children get a **pastel** (birthday cake) and may have a party with friends, family, balloons, presents, and a piñata. The morning of a Saint's Day or birthday starts with the song "Las Mañanitas." Later, girls may get a serenade.

Many towns and villages in Mexico hold parties to celebrate their patron saints. The festivities usually begin with a special church service held at the main Catholic Church named after the saint. Afterwards, there is usually music, food, and dancing. These are important days that townspeople look forward to all year.

Quinceañera

What will you do for your 15th birthday? Would you like to get dressed up, have a big party, and be the center of attention? For many Mexican girls, this isn't an ordinary birthday party. This party marks the turning from a child into an adult. After her **quinceañera**, a girl is treated as a woman.

The evening of the quinceañera starts with a mass. Afterwards a rich family may invite hundreds of friends for a formal dance. There they present their daughter to the community. A less wealthy family may have a party at home or invite the neighborhood over for **tamales** and **menudo** (a tripe soup). Families do their best to honor their 15-year-old daughters. On her quinceañera, a Mexican girl is queen!

Piñatas

Children love piñatas at birthday parties. Where did Mexican piñatas come from? Aztecs celebrated the birthday of Huitzilopochtli each December. They broke jars filled with treats and covered with feathers at the feet of his statue. But piñatas were also used in Europe before Europeans came to the Americas. Italian and Spanish children broke piñatas on the first Sunday of Lent. The idea of these piñatas may have come to Europe from China! Mexican piñatas may be a combination of Aztec and Spanish traditions.

Today **piñateros** (piñata makers) make piñatas in all shapes . . . vegetables, panda bears, bulls, and cartoon characters.

Huitzilopochtli, Blue Hummingbird, was the Aztec god of the sun and war. He was their special god. He made the sun come up every morning and demanded human blood to continue his work. Aztecs offered him the blood and hearts of victims they captured in war. Huitzilopochtli's statue was covered with gold and jewels.

Corpus Christi

A boy trots behind his mother through the crowded market. He stops in front of a row of little mules made from corn husks. The vendor smiles and picks one up. "Do you like it?" she asks. The child nods. The vendor puts the **mulita** (little mule) into the child's hands. He grins at the bright fruits and flowers loaded in the mulita's crates.

"**Hijo!** (Son!)" his mother calls.

"Over here," the vendor answers. "He wants a mulita."

His mother scolds him for stopping, then asks how much. Tomorrow is the celebration of Corpus Christi, and everyone loves the mulitas that fill the vendors' stands.

Children dress in traditional indígena outfits. Boys paint mustaches on their lips. Girls wrap doll babies in **rebozos** (shawls) to carry on their backs. Girls fill their arms with flowers and laquered trays of fruits. The boys load crates filled with tiny fruits and flowers on their backs. They carry their bright cargo through the streets to the church to be blessed.

Corpus Christi, which falls in late May or early June, celebrates the first fruits of summer. In Mexico City, streets are carpeted with flowers. Flowers decorate buildings and fill the procession. There are bullfights and dancing. Everyone has fun.

During colonial times, indígenas from all around gathered in Mexico City at Corpus Christi. Indígenas weren't allowed to use their ancient Middle American calendar. The Spanish substituted their own calendar with its special church holidays and celebrations. Corpus Christi, in the spring, was the time the Spanish collected taxes. Mule trains, packed with food and goods from the Pacific coast, arrived from Acapulco at fiesta time. A **tianguis,** or great market, filled the zócalo. People crowded the market, buying and selling.

Today, Mexicans remember the mule trains with mulitas. They celebrate Corpus Christi, or Day of the Mules, as Spanish and Indians did long ago.

On Corpus Christi in Suchiapa, Chiapas, a giant feathered snake called Gigantón parades through town along with the Bible's David, and white-faced clowns. They meet dancers dressed like jaguars in the road. The jaguars hop around pretending to attack iguanas that the clowns carry on strings. Gigantón, a plumed serpent, is a lot like the ancient Mexican god Quetzalcóatl.

27

La Danza de los Voladores

The Flying Dancers

A hundred-foot pole towers over the plaza at Papantla, Vera Cruz. It is for the **voladores'** (fliers) celebration during Corpus Christi. The tradition comes from Aztec times. The four fliers, who may dress like birds or in ribboned costumes, represent four sacred birds. Each bird flies to the four directions . . . east to the god of the sun, north to the god of the winds, west to the god of the earth, and south to the god of water.

Before they begin their flying dance, the voladores prepare the pole. They ask the forest god to forgive them for taking the tree, his child. They build a platform on top of the pole and string a vine ladder from bottom to top. They tie long ropes to the platform and prepare them to unwind, little by little, during the dance. When it's time to dance, the men bow to the four directions. They climb the pole and tie the ropes around their waists. Music plays. The voladores dive off the tower. The platform turns while the ropes slowly unwind. Centrifugal force keeps the men flying, around and around the pole, until they reach the ground. Each man wants to circle the tower 13 times before he touches the earth.

If all four men complete their 13 circles, the voladores fly once around the tower for each of the 52 years in the Aztec "bundle of years."

La Danza de los Voladores connects heaven and earth, past and present. Ancient codices, or books of pictures, show voladores long before the Spanish arrived in Mexico. Children who hope to be voladores begin learning to "fly" when they are eight or nine. They are the fliers of tomorrow.

Quetzalcóatl

Quetzalcóatl, one of the oldest Middle American gods, appears in creation myths and many legends. He is the plumed serpent god, named for the **quetzal**, a rare bird with long green feathers that lives in the Mexican mountains (Chiapas), and **cóatl** which means water snake in Mayan. Mayans, the people of Teotihuacán, Toltecs, and Aztecs all worshipped Quetzalcóatl. One of the Aztecs' four main gods, he ruled water, earth, and sky.

Something interesting happened to Quetzalcóatl's story in the time of the Toltecs. In 947, a real prince, Topiltzin, was born and took Quetzalcóatl's name. He led a heroic life and the story of the man, Topiltzin Quetzalcóatl, was permanently mixed with the ancient legends of the god Quetzalcóatl. After being orphaned, he was raised by priests of Quetzalcóatl and became the high priest of their god and the ruler of the Toltec people. Now he was called Topiltzin Quetzalcóatl. He founded the city, Tula, which became the center of the Toltec empire. He brought artists and craftsmen from all around to work in Tula.

At the time, Toltecs honored Tezcatlipoca, shining mirror, as their special god. Prince Topiltzin Quetzalcóatl wanted his people to take Quetzalcóatl as their supreme god. Topiltzin declared Quetzalcóatl, a god of life and corn, would be happy with sacrifices of flowers and snakes. He outlawed human sacrifice. But many people were loyal to the old ways. They drove Topiltzin Quetzalcóatl from the city. Legend says he went east to the Mayans where, known as Kukulcan, he ruled from 987 to 1000. Other stories say he ran to the sea and floated away on a raft, or burned up in a bright fire and became the planet Venus. These stories promised he would return from the east to reclaim his city, Tula, and defeat its enemies.

Legends say Prince Quetzalcóatl had light hair, pale skin, and blue eyes. Many indígenas thought Cortés was Quetzalcóatl returning from the east. After the Spanish conquest, some people claimed Topiltzin Quetzalcóatl had been a European who landed in Mexico, maybe even Saint James, the Apostle, or Santiago, who was patron of the Spanish army. Cortes' army brought the banner and the stories of Saint James to Mexico.

In Taos, New Mexico, on July 25 and 26, El Vivarón, a giant snake, parades through the streets. One child pushes his huge head along in a wheelbarrow while others run behind under Vivarón's cloth body. Like Quetzalcóatl, Vivarón is a powerful serpent. The fiesta honors Santiago, whose story was attached, along with Prince Topiltzín's, to the legend of Middle America's plumed serpent god.

TULA   QUETZALTEPEC · LUGAR DE QUETZALES

El Zócalo
The Market

In some villages in Michoacán, restaurant owners traditionally serve tiny food on tiny tables. They ask ridiculously high prices . . . but the customer pays with a piece of candy, gum, or his own tiny object. Bakers bake one-inch breads. Guitar makers sell mini-guitars, the furniture man, doll-size chairs. The fruit vendor sells tiny fruits, all for pretend money. Tiny markets let everyone have fun!

Indígenas met in markets to trade, talk, and worship long before Europeans came to Mexico. When Hernán Cortés entered the Aztec city, Tenochtitlán, he wrote to King Carlos V of Spain: "The city has many plazas, where they constantly buy and sell. There is a plaza . . . circled with doorways where more than 60,000 animals are traded. There are all kinds of markets for buying food, jewelry of gold and silver, brass, copper, tin, stone, bone, shells and feathers. . . . They sell rabbits, hares, deer, and small dogs that they raise to eat. . . . There are druggists who sell medicines to drink, ointments, and creams. There are barbershops . . . (and) restaurants. . . . In these markets they sell everything on earth. . . . There is so much I can't remember it all and there is more I cannot name."

Today's markets are festive places where people shop, bargain, buy treats, or stroll on a warm evening. Every town has its zócalo (town square) where families and friends gather in the evening to walk and visit. Mexicans call this "dar paseo." You might buy cold melons, fresh-cut sugar cane, or sizzling **chicharrones** (fried pigs' skin). Children love long, cinnamon-sprinkled pastries, **churros**. A band may play in the gazebo. Markets and the zócalo make daily life festive. In Mexico, you don't need a holiday to meet your friends or to have a special treat.

But at fiesta time people pour into cities and villages from all around. They set up stalls selling crafts and treats along the zócalo. Pilgrims may buy **velas** (special large candles) to carry in a procession to the village church. Families buy fireworks and flowers. Folks from the countryside bargain for things they need to take home. Musicians serenade and children dart through the crowd selling gum and candies. Everyone is excited. The market, the zócalo, and the church are the center of celebrations.

Tamales de Dulce
Sweet Tamales

In Mexico, making tamales is a family affair. Mothers, grandmothers, aunts, cousins, nieces, and good friends get together to have a fun day in the kitchen. They prepare tamales for festivals and celebrations. While most tamales are filled with meat, some are sweet and eaten for dessert. Your local Mexican market or international food store will have corn husks and *masa harina*. This recipe makes about 40 tamales. Tamales freeze very well.

> 1 cup (½ lb.) lard
> 3 cups *masa harina* (dehydrated corn flour—do not substitute)
> canned peaches, pineapple, or apricots, puréed to make 1¼ cups
> ½ cup sugar
> 1 teaspoon salt
> 1½ teaspoons baking powder
> about 2 tablespoons juice from the canned fruit if dough is too stiff to spread easily
> 60 dried corn husks

Whip lard with electric mixer or spoon until light and fluffy. Blend in the masa, fruit purée, sugar, salt, baking powder, and fruit juice if necessary. Soak 50 to 60 corn husks in warm water until they are soft. Remove any corn silk and dirt. Wash well and drain. Don't worry if they split. Two small ones can be overlapped and used as one. Cover them to keep moist and soft.

Filling the tamales:
Lay a wide corn husk flat on the table with the tip away from you. Spread 1½ tablespoons of masa mix on the husk in a rectangle. Leave a little space on the left, but go all the way to the edge on the right. Fold the right side over to the center of the filling. Fold the left side over that. Fold the bottom end up part way and then fold the top down. Lay the folded side down to keep it closed.

Steaming the tamales (about one hour):
Place a rack above 2 inches of water in a pot. Stack the tamales on the rack, folded side down. Arrange them loosely so they will cook evenly. Cover the kettle, bring to a boil, and cook over medium heat so the water boils gently. Check from time to time to be sure there is still water in the pot. The cooking time depends on how many tamales you have stacked in the steamer. After one hour, take one out from the middle of the stack and open it. If the dough is firm, does not taste raw or doughy, and does not stick to the husk, they are done.

Hungry Boy and the Corn Maiden

At the end of summer, many indígena people traditionally celebrate the harvest. Huichol people, who live in the states of Jalisco and Nayarit, bless the five colors of corn and their children in a fall celebration, the Corn and Drum Ceremony. One of their stories of how they received corn goes like this:

Long ago, in the time of the animal people, a mother and her son, Hungry Boy, were always starving. One day he said, "I've heard maize grows on the other side of the mountain. I'll go bring back corn."

Hungry Boy walked and walked until at last he saw people. They said, "Come with us, we're looking for maize too." But they were animal people who could change into animals. That night, while he slept, they changed to ants and ate his clothes and hair, even his eyebrows and eyelashes.

Hungry Boy woke alone and hungry. "Where are my clothes? Where is my hair, my eyebrows, my eyelashes? At least they left my bow and arrows."

He hunted for food, and aimed his arrow at a white dove. But she was one of the nature ancestors. She said, "Don't shoot. I'm your Mother Dove."

"Mother Dove, I didn't recognize you. I'm hungry and can't find food. My mother is hungry too."

Then Mother Dove asked him five times, "Are you so hungry it hurts?"

Five times he answered, "I'm so hungry my stomach hurts."

Mother Dove took him home and fed him from a gourd bowl that never emptied. He ate and ate, until, ashamed, he said, "Mother Dove, I've eaten too much. I thought there wouldn't be enough food for me."

"My son," she explained, "I am guardian of the maize." Then she called for her beautiful daughters, White Corn Maiden, Yellow Corn Maiden, Red Corn Maiden, Speckled Corn Maiden, and Blue Corn Maiden. Mother Dove said, "You shall marry one of my daughters."

At first, the girls giggled and didn't want to leave home. Then Blue Corn Maiden said, "I would be honored to marry Hungry Boy."

Mother Dove warned Hungry Boy, "Care for your wife. Tell your mother that Blue Corn Maiden must never grind corn or help make tortillas. Make her a special place in your mother's house. If you promise this there will be plenty of corn in your home. Otherwise, sorrow and hunger will return."

"I promise, Mother Dove."

They married. On the journey home, Hungry Boy's wife had hot tortillas ready for him each night. He asked, "How do you make these tortillas?"

She answered, "It is who I am . . . corn."

Arriving home, Hungry Boy hurried in. "Mother, I brought a wife. She is corn. Please, don't ask her to work. She can never, never help cook corn or make tortillas. Promise."

Hungry Boy's mother gasped, "How can you bring someone else to feed, no food, and now a wife who can't even work!"

"Mother, I'll work in the fields," he answered.

So Mother-in-Law let her daughter-in-law in the house. That night, corn blew into every bowl and storage box. In the morning, all the containers bulged with corn. Hungry Boy made a special place for Blue Corn Maiden to sit on a ledge, out of the way. Then he went to work in the fields.

The first day Mother-in-Law worked silently. But each day Mother-in-law got more angry. By the fifth day she grumbled, "It's not fair. I do all the work while the beautiful one sits so pretty!"

Blue Corn Maiden felt terrible. She jumped down. "Let me help. You work hard. I am young and you are old. You should rest." But when Blue Corn Maiden started grinding corn, she began to disappear. She was grinding herself away! She made tortillas and put them on the griddle, but she couldn't remove her burning hand. She cried with pain as the wind began to blow.

Hungry Boy burst inside and grabbed his wife's dress but it was too late. The fierce wind blew Blue Corn Maiden away. All that was left was a piece of her embroidered sleeve. Then his mother screamed, "There is no more corn!"

Hungry Boy saw it was true. "My wife is gone, and she took the corn with her. I'll go find her." He traveled to Mother Dove's home and asked, "May I have my wife back?"

"No," she answered. "You couldn't care for her. It isn't easy to grow corn. Now you must work hard. Sometimes you'll have corn and sometimes you won't. Go home, Hungry Boy. I can't help you because you didn't take care of the gift I gave you."

Mother Dove's words were true. The Huicholes work hard growing corn. They know corn and children are life. If cared for tenderly, both may flower, grow, and survive into the future.

Independence Day

It is dark in Mexico City. It is late. Families bundle children into coats and sweaters. In September, high up in Mexico City, night can be cold. Tonight, no one cares. Families come from all corners of the city. They arrive from out of town. As midnight gets closer, more and more people fill the streets. They walk in small groups, then in a stream, until they join the crowd filling the zócalo. Hundreds of thousands of people have come for one moment . . . midnight of Mexican Independence Day.

Fireworks flash. Flags wave. Everyone waits in the jammed zócalo. There he is. The president and his family step onto the balcony at the National Palace. He waves. The crowd quiets. The president rings a bell, then lifts his hands and shouts ¡VIVA MÉXICO! Long live Mexico!

¡VIVA! the crowd shouts back, ¡VIVA MÉXICO! The president shouts again. ¡Viva México! they reply. Goose bumps tingle on women's arms. Children perch on their fathers' shoulders to see. ¡Viva Hidalgo! The president cries again, ¡Viva! the crowd yells louder, ¡Viva Allende! ¡Viva Aldama! **¡Vivan los héroes que nos dieron patria!** (Long live the heroes who gave us our country) they shout.

This is the **Grito de Dolores,** the cry for independence Mexicans will always remember. They repeat it, at midnight every September 15 in Mexico City's zócalo. The scene is the same in every state capital, in Morelia, Monterrey, Oaxaca, in small towns across the country. The highest official rings the bell to remember Father Hidalgo and the crowd gives the Grito. Parents bring their children to feel the thrill of shouting with the crowd, of celebrating independence, and of being Mexican.

After the Grito, the crowd wanders back down the streets. Vendors sell cotton candy, corn, and sweets from sidewalk stalls. Children line up to take a ride on a ferris wheel. Fireworks explode. It is a grand celebration.

In the United States, there are celebrations in Chicago, Los Angeles and other cities on Independence Day. Mexican Americans may throw parties at their homes on September 15, shouting the **Grito** at midnight. There are also big parades and fiestas held around the United States for **Cinco de Mayo,** Fifth of May. This holiday honors the Battle of Puebla, May 5, 1862. On that day, Mexican farmers and workers armed mostly with sticks and machetes won a battle against the powerful French army that had invaded Mexico.

Independence

Mexicans chose to show this Aztec legend on their flag: Aztecs roamed central Mexico for a long time looking for a place to live. Finally, their god, Huitzilopochtli, told them he would turn himself into an eagle. They should build a village where they found the eagle sitting on a cactus eating a snake. They saw the eagle on an island in Lake Texcoco. Aztecs settled there. Their village became the great city, Tenochtitlán, the place of the cactus. Modern Mexico City is in the same place.

Spanish conquerors used indígenas to work the land and the mines. Indígenas could not own land or move easily. People born to Spanish and indígena parents were called **mestizos**. They could not be community leaders or do certain jobs. At first, mestizos were indígenas without a tribe and Spaniards without power. No one wanted them. As more and more Mexicans were born mestizos, they became a hard-working poor class. Indígenas and mestizos had three hundred years to learn to hate the Spanish.

Another group resented the Spanish. They were **criollos**, Spanish who were born in Mexico. Although they had many privileges, they were not allowed to have real power. Spanish rulers gave important jobs to people born in Spain. In 1810, criollos across Mexico plotted a revolution. They planned to declare independence in December.

But in mid-September, the Spanish uncovered their plot. The revolutionaries decided to make their move.

Early on Sunday, September 16, 1810, Father Hidalgo, one of the leaders, rang the church bells in Dolores, Guanajuato. When the people gathered, he spoke from his church steps. He said the time had come to fight the Spanish. The time had come for Mexicans to be free. The crowd responded with a great shout . . . el Grito de Dolores.

Hidalgo organized an army of poor indígenas and mestizos to fight the Spanish. He declared African slaves in Mexico to be free . . . the first declaration of freedom for slaves in the Americas. His army, sometimes armed with only sticks and arrows, fought until the Spanish captured Father Hidalgo, and rebel army officers Allende and Aldama and executed them. But the Mexican people continued to fight for 11 years until they gained their independence in 1821.

Among the many heroes of the uprising are women. Josefa Ortiz de Domínguez put the revolution in motion by warning Hidalgo the Spanish had uncovered their plot, and Doña Leona Vicario risked her life and fortune to send supplies and information to the rebels.

Independence Day is celebrated on September 16, the day Hidalgo started a revolution in Dolores. ¡Viva México!

Papel Picado
Cut Paper

Look up. It's fiesta time. Brightly colored decorations hang across village streets. Rows of green, blue, purple, orange, and yellow paper flutter in the wind. Sheets of finely cut, colored tissue paper arranged in bright patterns are glued side by side onto strings. Overhead, line after line of **papel picado** reflects the colors of the fiesta. You can make papel picado:

You will need colored tissue paper cut in squares or rectangles, scissors, string, and glue.

Fold the tissue in half, then quarters, and eighths as though you are making snow flakes.

Cut designs into the edges of the folded paper, being careful not to cut off the whole folded edge. Leave the corners square, or nearly square. After cutting your paper, unfold it carefully. Fold over the top of each piece just enough to wrap around a long string. When you have 10 or 20 pieces, arrange them along the string. Glue or staple them to make a long banner. Hang it up. Make another. **¡Qué lindo es!** How pretty!

La Frontera

The Frontier

During the Mexican American War the U.S. Army was fighting its way through Mexico City. Six teenage boys chose to die fighting rather than surrender their military school. They say some boys wrapped themselves in the Mexican flag and jumped from the fortress walls to their deaths. Today, September 13, the day **Los Niños Héroes de Chapultepec** (The Boy Heroes of Chapultepec) died, is a national holiday in Mexico.

A calf darts across the ring. Hooves pound behind him, a dust cloud rises. The lariat whistles and the calf falls. The crowd cheers. The rider waves. He's not any rodeo cowboy. He's a **vaquero**. Mexicans, from Guadalajara to Vera Cruz, enjoy **charreadas**, Mexican rodeos. Left over from the days when vaqueros raised cattle on Mexico's northern frontier, charreadas were the first rodeos.

Mexican vaqueros (cowboys) followed herds through northern Mexico and what is now the southwestern United States. They invented the **la reata** (lariat), and the **jáquima** (hackamore), talked about broncos and corrals, and dispayed their skills in charreadas. Vaqueros taught cowboys in the United States and Canada the Mexican ways of roping and breaking horses.

Vaqueros fought bravely for Mexico's freedom. They became a symbol of Mexican independence. The Mexicans who fought for freedom from Spain no longer felt Spanish. Many of them weren't indígena either. They were mestizos. On Mexico's northern frontier, indígenas and mestizos, who were treated poorly in cities, could work hard and get ahead. They started **ranchos** (ranches) or worked as vaqueros. These men and women weren't Spanish or indígena. They were purely Mexican.

Land and Liberty:

The Second Revolution

The leaders of 1810 were dead by the time Mexico won its independence in 1821. Children and grandchildren of the Spanish, criollos, became the new rulers. They didn't want to give land back to the indígenas or let mestizos share their privileges. They spent years fighting bloody battles over who would control Mexico.

The next decades were filled with wars, invasions, and hardship. The United States provoked the Mexican American War (1846–1848) and took half of Mexico's land (Texas, Arizona, New Mexico, Utah, Colorado, Nevada, California, and part of Wyoming). Civil war tore Mexico between 1858 and 1861. The French invaded in 1862, sending Austrian Prince, Maximilian, to rule the country.

In 1867, Mexicans, led by President Benito Juárez, an indígena from Oaxaca, reclaimed their nation. Juárez executed Maximilian. When Juárez died, his rival, Porfirio Díaz took over. Díaz ruled Mexico for 34 years (1876–1910). He encouraged foreign countries to build factories and railroads in Mexico, but most of the profit went to those countries. Both Juárez' and Díaz' governments took land owned by indígena communities and sold it to large landholders. Díaz didn't let people question his government. Mexico was modernizing but people's lives got worse.

In 1910, a second revolution broke out. Díaz had allowed elections. Although many people voted for Francisco I. Maderos, Díaz announced that 99% of the people voted for him. Maderos fought to be president. Indígenas in Morelos, led by Emiliano Zapata, fought to regain their land. Pancho Villa, a colorful northern vaquero, loaded men and horses on trains and fought up and down northern Mexico. Álvaro Obregón's disciplined army of Yaquí indígenas battled from Sonora to Mexico City. Díaz fled the country. Maderos was murdered. The rebels won in 1914. This revolution was about more than who was president. People demanded change.

After 1910 there was more opportunity, especially for mestizos. The government did take some land from large landholders and give it to peasants. But generals, political leaders, and their armies fought each other for years. Instead of land and liberty, most Mexicans got hardship and bloodshed. It was 30 years before things got better.

In the violent years following the Mexican Revolution, one tenth of Mexico's population moved permanently across the U.S.–Mexico border. After the United States entered World War II in 1941, more Mexicans were recruited to fill jobs in Chicago, Detroit, and other U.S. cities. After the war, a law allowed many Mexicans to do farm work in the United States. These workers, **braceros**, labored during the harvest season and then were sent back to Mexico. Wages were low, but better than in Mexico. Life for braceros was hard. They lived in crowded housing, and got poor medical care. Many died from accidents and overwork. The bracero program was cancelled in 1964 but many farms in the West continued to rely on Mexican workers to pick their crops.

El Día de los Muertos

Day of the Dead

Can you imagine eating candy skulls, spending the night at a cemetery, or preparing special food for a dead relative? These are things Mexican children look forward to on **El Día de los Muertos**, the Day of the Dead. It's not a spooky time, like Halloween. Los Días de los Muertos (November 1 and 2) is a time to celebrate and honor the dead. Ancient Mexicans believed dead people moved on to a different world. Death was another kind of living. Spanish priests, wanting to replace the indígena religion with the Catholic one, tried to stop the people's celebrations for the dead. When that didn't work, they combined the traditions with the ancient Catholic holy days for the dead, All Souls and All Saints Days, on November 1 and 2.

During the last week of October, markets fill with foods, flowers, and toys for celebrating El Día de los Muertos. You can buy **pan de los muertos** (bread for the dead) or **calaveras de azúcar** (sugar skulls). Children love to eat them and to give them to their friends. As El Día de los Muertos gets closer, homes fill with the smells of chocolate and chiles. Everyone cooks special foods like tamales and chicken mole. They gather the food and flowers they will need to celebrate.

On November 1 and 2, whole families get together to clean and decorate their relatives' graves. They make paths of marigolds or candles to guide the spirits. They build altars at churches and graveyards. Each altar is different. The family arranges marigolds, candles, incense, and a photo of the dead person on an embroidered tablecloth. They add fruits, flowers, and the dead person's favorite foods. They decorate graves of dead children with sugar skulls, toys, and Mexican chocolate.

On the night of November 1, everyone meets at the graveyard. Many Mexicans believe that spirits return that night to meet with the living. They take food for everyone, including the dead. It is an exciting time . . . a time to remember aunts and grandparents, a time to feel their presence, a time to be together with all the family, living and dead.

"It is perhaps true
one lives on earth.
But not forever on earth,
just a little while here.
Although it is jade,
it breaks.
Although it is gold,
it breaks.
Although it is
quetzal feathers,
it tears.
Not forever on earth,
just a little while here."

—*Náhuatl poem*

Un Cuento de Teotitlán

A Story of Teotitlán

There was a woman in Teotitlán who didn't believe in spirits. Her husband had to leave home before El Día de los Muertos. He said, "Prepare an altar to honor my mother and father. And make your best mole, to welcome them since I will be gone."

The woman didn't believe the spirits would return. She didn't make an altar. Instead she set out bricks. She didn't make mole. She killed a turkey and ate it all by herself.

On his way home, her husband met the spirits of his dead parents. "Where was our offering?" they demanded. "Why did you make us sad by ignoring us on our day?"

The husband was furious. But his spirit parents told him not to scold his wife. Instead they said, "Tell her to go to mass wearing her new clothes from the chest in the corner."

The next morning his wife jumped out of bed, happy to go to mass in her fine new clothes. But when she opened the chest, what a shock! All her lovely clothes were printed with skulls and bones. Within minutes, she was dead. Now the whole village of Teotitlán tells her story.

Esqueletos y Calaveras
Skeletons and Skulls

Skeletons aren't scary to Mexicans. They are funny. At El Día de los Muertos, children can buy little scenes of skeletons going to school, getting a haircut, or getting married. There are all kinds of skeleton puppets and toy skeletons that move every which way. There are even skeleton jokes! No wonder. Mictlantecuhtli, the Aztec god of death, was a skeleton with a smile! People write **calaveras** (skull jokes) about living people and put them in the newspaper. One said, "I already saw your skull with your four teeth and one molar." This calavera was written about a famous potter, Teodora Blanco.

> Al estar haciendo un jarro
> a Teodora sorprendió
> la parca y la convertió
> en muñequito de barro.
>
> One day she was making a pot
> When death came paying a call,
> He startled Teodora
> And turned her to a clay doll.

Pan de los Muertos y Chocolate Caliente
Bread for the Dead and Hot Chocolate

In October and early November, look for loaves of **pan de los muertos** at **panaderías** (Mexican bakeries). You'll recognize them by their dough decorations . . . little birds, spirit people, or other figures on top, and braid around the edges. Flavored with orange and anise (licorice), pan de los muertos is delicious with Mexican hot chocolate.

Middle Americans considered chocolate a drink for important people and gods. They used cocoa beans as a kind of money and drank chocolate on special occasions. You can buy blocks of Mexican chocolate in many supermarkets. It is made of chocolate, vanilla, almond, and cinnamon, and comes in colorful boxes. Follow the instructions on the box. Try using a traditional **molinillo** (beater) to make your chocolate foam!

Dancing Jaguars and Little Old Men

In Acatlán, Puebla, children carry marigolds and candies for the dead. They stop outside the cemetery. The youngest ones peek from behind their parents' knees. Older ones squeal with delight as dancers dressed like jaguars, devils, skeletons, and **rancheros viejos** (old farmers) pull them from the crowd. It is all for fun and to honor the dead.

In Michoacán, men and boys dress up like old men and totter around holding their backs in **La Danza de los Viejitos** (Dance of the Old Men). They dance slowly at first, making careful, painful steps. Suddenly young again, they leap and turn like athletes. The dance ends with the men hobbling around, viejitos once more. Ancient sculptures show Huehueteotl, the Aztec god of fire, as a bent over old man carrying a charcoal burner on his back. La Danza de los Viejitos originally honored this old-man god.

Marigolds are called **cempasúchil** or **Flor de los Muertos,** Flower of the Dead. They have been used for the dead in Mexico since ancient times. People decorate tombs, altars, and pathways with marigolds at El Día de los Muertos. They mark paths from children's graves to their homes with marigold petals. That way children's spirits won't get lost on the way home. You can make your own design by gluing marigold, other flower petals, or corn kernels onto cardboard. Try designing skulls, skeletons, or bones.

Something to Celebrate

Children in Mexican communities in the United States from Texas to California make paper flowers, skeletons, and altars for El Día de Los Muertos. In San Francisco's Mission District, people dress up like skeletons and carry candles in a procession through the streets. Community altars in shop windows reflect the memories and hopes of families and the whole community. The arrangements of skulls, family photos, and skeletons are often crowned with a picture of La Virgen de Guadalupe—Mexico's special patron!

All kinds of people look to La Virgen de Guadalupe for help and support throughout the year. Her picture hangs in Mexican homes, on buses, and in cars. She appears in statues in churches and plazas, and in murals on building walls.

Wrapped in a cloak of stars, the Virgin with her dark hair and eyes, is seen not only as Jesus' mother, but as a mother to native people. She is Mexico's protector. When Father Hidalgo declared Mexican independence in 1810, his flag was a banner of La Virgen de Guadalupe. Emiliano Zapata's troops carried her banner in 1910. Years later, in 1965, when the great union leader César Chávez led California farm workers in a struggle for fair pay for their work, they marched behind a banner of La Virgen de Guadalupe.

Mexican people take strength from different worlds. In Mexico, ancient pyramids and colonial churches stand next to skyscrapers. Some women pat out tortillas while others make computer chips. The foods, dances, spirit, and pride passed down from indígenas continue in Mexico. So does the faith, language, and gaiety of the Spanish. But the work of the revolution is not done. Farmers still wait for land taken from them long ago. Profits from Mexico's resources—oil and minerals—don't help enough people. As the population grows, more people need more schools, jobs, and land. Many people must leave villages to find work. Some cross the border to the United States to work in the fields and cities. They join communities of Mexican Americans who have lived in the United States for generations.

Mexican Americans are proud of their rich culture. They balance their Mexican heritage with their North American lives. Mexican Americans know the importance of language and tradition for a people. They treasure their customs, their families, and their Spanish language. They continue to work for fair treatment, better jobs, and opportunities for their children.

Today Mexican culture is part of American life. Do you like tacos? Do you break a piñata at your birthday or Christmas? Have you been to a rodeo? Maybe you use words like **gracias, adiós**, and **hasta luego**. Maybe you celebrate Cinco de Mayo or El Día de los Muertos at your school. You are sharing a little of Mexico. Every time we share, we learn more about each other. Then Mexicans, Mexican Americans, and other North Americans have something special to celebrate.

Like precious gifts from the Tres Reyes or offerings of flowers for La Virgen de Guadalupe, Mexicans bring gifts to the future . . . the courage of their ancestors, the strength of their communities, and the dreams of their children. The heart of Mexico is its people, wherever they live.

Glossary

agua de frutas: fruit water, a sweet fruit drink
aguinaldos: Christmas treats wrapped in special papers
biscochitos: little cookies, traditional New Mexican Christmas cookies
balero: a popular wooden cup-and-ball toy
bracero: a Mexican worker allowed in the United States under a special work program
buñuelos: fried sweet Christmas bread
calaveras: skulls
cascarones: egg shells
cohetes: firework rockets
comadre: godmother
criollos: people born to Spanish parents in Mexico
charreada: Mexican rodeo
chicharrónes: fried pigs' skin
chinampas: Aztecs' floating fields
chocolate caliente: hot chocolate
churros: fried sweet pastry
dar paseo: to take a walk
disfrute: enjoy
encantado: enchanted
esqueletos: skeletons
¡Feliz Navidad!: Merry Christmas!
grito: shout
guitarrones: large guitars
hijo, hija: son, daughter
indígenas: original or native people
jáquima: hackamore, a type of horse bridle
luminarias: traditional Christmas lights
menudo: traditional tripe soup

mestizo: a person with Spanish and indígena ancestors
mole: a spicy Mexican sauce made with chocolate
molinillo: traditional chocolate beater
mulitos: little mules
nacimientos: manger scenes
pan de los muertos: bread of the dead
panadería: bakery
paragüeros: umbrella salesmen
peregrinos: pilgrims
piñateros: people who make piñatas
posada: traditional Christmas procession
quinceañera: a party celebrating a 15-year-old girl's beginning adulthood
rábanos: radishes
La Rama: the branch, traditional Christmas activity
raspada: snow cone
rebozo: traditional shawl
la reata: lariat, lasso
rosca de reyes: bread for Three Kings Day
tamales: traditional dish made of filled, steamed corn meal, wrapped in corn husks
Semana Santa: Holy Week
tianguis: market
tilma: a cloak
tortas: cakes or sandwiches
vaquero: cowboy
velas: candles
¡Viva!: Long live!
voladores: fliers
zócalo: town square or plaza

Tijuana

Mexicali

Ensenada

Baja
California
Norte

San
Quintin

Puerto
Penasco

Nogales

Ciudad
Juarez

Sonora

Chihuahua

Ojinaga

Hermosillo

Chihuahua

Guaymas

Delicias

Isla
Cedros

Santa Rosalia

Cuidad
Obregon

Hidalgo
del Parral

Gulf of
California

Loreto

Los Mochis

Torreon

Baja
California
Sur

Culiacan

Durango

La Paz

Sinaloa

Durango

San Lucas

Mazatlan

North
Pacific
Ocean

Nayarit

Islas
Marias

Tepic

Guadalajara

Jalisco

Colima

Colima

Manzanillo